THE STEEL VEIL

THE STEEL VEIL

POEMS

JACK MARSHALL

COFFEE HOUSE PRESS · MINNEAPOLIS · 2008

COFFEE HOUSE PRESS books are available to the trade through our primary distributor, Consortium Book Sales & Distribution, www.cbsd.com or (800) 283-3572. For personal orders, catalogs, or other information, write to: Coffee House Press, 27 North Fourth Street, Suite 400, Minneapolis, MN 55401.

Coffee House Press is a nonprofit literary publishing house. Support from private foundations, corporate giving programs, government programs, and generous individuals helps make the publication of our books possible. We gratefully acknowledge their support in detail in the back of this book.

To you and our many readers around the world, we send our thanks for your continuing support.

LIBRARY OF CONGRESS CIP INFORMATION

Marshall, Jack, 1936–
The steel veil : poems / by Jack Marshall.
p. cm.
ISBN 978-1-56689-220-9 (alk. paper)
I. Title.
PS3563.A722S74 2008
811'.54—DC22
2008012530

ACKNOWLEDGMENTS

Several of these poems appeared originally in the following magazines:
*The Café Review, The Common Review, Exquisite Corpse,
Perigee* (online), *The Forward, Talisman, Tarpaulin Sky* (online),
Today's Alternative News (online), and *Zyzzyva.*

I would also like to give thanks to Naomi Schwartz and Chris Fischbach
for their editorial care and assistance with this book.

For Naomi,
and in memory of Renee Marshall Zwirn

Contents

PART 3

PART 4

PART 5

PART 1

DIMMING

There is a glacier, grown slowly as hair,
dissolving faster than our thoughts
run past. There is one's self, close

to being absent at any moment, and all
of us under a sign in an unknown season
we know for certain we'll be dying,

when loved ones will vanish, and we
unable to hold or kiss or ever miss them again.

Besides warming, there's the double whammy
of global dimming: obstructed solar rays
the red rim on the blackening tin twilight is riding,

like the slowed-down sweeping of a grain
of glucose firing through the brain, the way
memory comes from, into, and through

what we feel, and becomes real;
like the past, inventing itself in the last second
I keep coming back to the places that keep

coming from the sunset I am a student of
at my desk, where every seat is front-row;
the vast red vapor trail erasing the horizon

against which time narrows and place deepens
in the clarity of outline, in the last light.

I am a student of sinking that lasts
seconds, and of which I am a part, and
do not follow. The longer I fail, the longer

I live. To live, I fail; I fail, and live
in the furrows of feelings that live
in the places we lived in, empty now

of us and what we did there,
with failing faith, failed friends, in moments
that were loved, in hours that weren't.

WHILE I DISMANTLE THE HOUSE, POETRY GOES PACKING

Going out the door, you never know
what's in store in the never-thought-about
that now needs rethinking on the white road
as always running nowhere.

"Everything east of me I already know." —
Who said that? Where are they now?
And taking pen in hand doesn't part
the way to the long view that serenely looks
through the trash that passes, the mass
graves that grow.

          I can't
remember what it was good for. Was it
only for the accuracy
in the foreboding:
when something awful happens,
and we knew it would?
Something I feel unreturnable
goes out of me. I wonder
what it was good for.

"Should we take poetry seriously at all? Tell me
yes, give me reasons," I hear
the old poet plead, forlorn, insistent
as the last ho-ho bird on Oahu
whistling his mating call for years
to a female of the species long extinct.

For the life of me, I wonder
what it was I thought
it was ever good for.

WHAT I'M DOING HERE

July is waving its wine-red wand
at the gore that has come
to stay. I put another Sunday
behind me; another
doomsday before.

Growing old in the crib
of my rib cage,
in the munificent living
larder of the Lord,
in the luxury of later
(banning a black so bleak
holding blindness in store),
what I'm doing here
has nothing to do with
what I've known before,
or where it began.
What I'm doing here
when night melts its moist
mouth in my ear, is hearing
the hummingbird
whirring I've wanted
to ride out of sight.

PULL

Growing older, feeling a greater pull
into a deeper way
than the physical,
I turn the nozzle spray's

mist and aim at the flowerbed.
A hummingbird, red-throated,
needle-beaked ruby, flits down
from jabbing the overhead blossoms.

Wings beating a rainbow blur play
me and the mist to its tiny heart's ferment;
darts off to the edge of the spray,
then away, to higher blossoms in sibilant

spasmodic ticks. Small buds
and dirt-bombs I pick up and throw
against the fence to chase with thuds
the squirrel who's turned a glaring eye

down on my cats—such surprise
stuns their ten eager upturned eyes!—
to save its brash, wagging tail. Writing this,
of hooks and links and locked eyes,

folds me into—I don't know why—
my father's swift flowing Arabic calligraphy.

Apologies to the Spider

A thread glistening across the archway
blocks my entry to the garden. Should I
duck, or break it? I duck,
and still break it. Would that luck

were otherwise, I get
close up and personal
to a ragged webbed spiral,
as if a galaxy's thumbprint were set

in silk, and I'm caught
like a thief without anything
to steal but seeds, bugs, wings,
and left with not much heart

to plead innocence. And talk
about ambition!—Lean one way,
and see it shimmer; lean another, and see
a woven world we move through, break. Look

again: An angel-hair
plumb line—anchored fence-top to rose-tip
ten feet apart, (how could it swing so far
out?)—makes it

short of flying through space
in a grid less secure
than thread. My cat Charlie's face,
as he wobbles toward me, is a blur:

cobweb-whiskers snagged in mist-gray
hedges where webs are thickest. We move,
each on our separate frequency,
on a trellis of nerve-

ends through which impulses cross synapse,
or fall in the gaps.

In This Ring of Boundless Ripples

Light as our green-eyed cat's step
  on the new spring grass, morning air
    stirs, variously scented, no breeze but

with a flower's fragrance passes,
  as does the wailing sound heading into
    summer of the freight train approaching,

then passing, which may have wailed
  as well in winter but, closed down,
    I hadn't listened.

Paying attention is the hardest payment
  to make: each day I am living
    proof. And on the streets

of little tenderness, thronged as causeways
  to cemeteries waiting for the clinching
    detail, in a driven, fissured world,

we value nothing so much as what we are about
  to lose, that we grasp
    at the last. I know

such testaments of the aged—
   Asphodel, Four Quartets, The Rock,
      Hardy, Jeffers, Oppen—that flower

near the end, for us might be
   any day now.
      Whether we've been mean

or merciful, rain has been
   pumping the blueberries into plump,
      succulent clusters beneath their sheen

of powdery dust. To make that
   last awareness day's first,
      and not forget

the berries' blueness beneath their dust; the dress
   of rose petals spread on the ground;
      your headlamp in the garden at night,

a miner's high-beamed eye
   tracking aphids and snails down
      with plucked precision.

The gardener's "green thumb" outdone
   by your green arm often running red
      from thorns you'd almost give CPR

to revive. "Roses are forgiving,"
    you say, but to me they're pitiless
        as the claws of our cats I call "ungrateful"

(especially the feral tabby I rescued,
    who couldn't care less),
        when you comb, clip, and groom them

in fierce, focused embrace.
    I have cut back the strangling
        nightshade vines, for now. In the infinite

ring of boundless ripples, there are places
    with more of what there is of
        here. We have worked to make the boundless

near; have chosen this ring
    to live in, that the fist
        of each self unclench

to make, of noon a shaded garden, and evening, shelter.

Courtesy

The blind man I help onto the bus
tells me, "I took the bus to see
my mother. She doesn't get out much.
We watched football on TV."
I note he keeps his ones and fives
in different pockets of his wallet
as he fingers them to pay the fare.
I glance out the window. "It looks
like rain," I say. We cross a bridge;
fog hazes, a lighthouse beams
in the distance. At my stop,
I get up to leave. "See you later,"
he says, facing straight ahead.
And I sense it as a courtesy,
his speaking my language
of saying more than we can see.

Predator of Perception

Thread to thread, gap to gap,
schizy as a spider mending its trap-

ezoidal web, he pauses in the late evening mist
of early old age, fixed

to steer the wrong turns right. Rust
would do the rest.

In time, as beautiful turns brutal, and pointed
is blunted,

as claws in the meadows
inch up the beam to the gallows,

though no mouth is big enough
to utter the whole premature leaf-

fall of late bloom, he wonders
what he started out for

before the restless sleepwalk drained
childhood away; how far beyond

where he had thought so long ago
he'd reach, at rest, by now?

Heard enough, seen enough,
too late for lessons in how to bluff

making up for lost time.
To deaden dying, let him

gather his powers, like rust.
Gathering in secret is best.

ANOTHER WAY

Ranging wide as blue given a sky
for a jay's piercing cry

to deepen in, memory brings her holding
an apple, the ripe rind's uncoiling

flower, fanning out, falling away
from the paring knife. Drained day's

chores done, in her fist a shiny globe,
plump pick of McIntosh, she lobs

the browning skein's unbroken loop
brushing the floor before it drops,

accordion-ringed, into the sink. Though it's
tightly wound around us, we miss

home when it's shed, thinking, wrongly,
the future will be a repetition already

familiar. Whoever reads me now
shares another way

of being alone.

BRIEFEST BLOSSOM

There are days that seem like heaven
might fall to earth and appear
as the life-to-come the unborn wait on
and the dying cling to. . . . Here,

today is not one of them. Magic
still to be made—
alluring, elusive as a virgin maid
who won't abide your logic—

is sudden
reversal of expectation,
full-blown subversion
with free run

of the house. No order
abiding from this time
on; no chance fortune nor earned failure,
but wayward whim

cutting through
gardens not meant to last; that blows
you kisses and crises
in more or less

unequal measure, exceeding surprise.
For other than this,
look to heaven's
briefest blossom.

LAYERS

As our outermost layer of skin cells is oldest,
Dead already, about to be shed
And mixed with the scales of the past,

Flesh made speech telling
The brutal tale of its time, tells it,
As always, reeling . . .

It's cold, it's hot,
It's east, it's west,
Barefoot, in boots,

Wherever the rush to ruin poses
As Holy Writ, the first
God, Chaos, runs his turbulence through us.

It must be so
The future not go
Unlived that it hides from view

The blood-ties binding the living, never realized,
Yet at times as though from another life
Recalled and, again for the last time, seized,

Then lost, like all the old houses and boarders
That vanished, with all the old summers in them,
On faded red-brick shoulders

All the warm-blooded bodies
Cast into cold
Katabatic skies.

MINT

In the garden, spiky mint,
You brush it back, release its scent;

Follow sundown out of time,
And note the shadows, and their climb.

Words you mouthed as lately yours,
Now you know were nothing more.

A fine-liner, a hair's breadth,
Draws twilight to evening berth.

In the garden, spiky mint,
You brush it back, release its scent.

PART 2

"Close to God"

"Close to God" is easy to say;
  to harness like a draft horse
  is harder. This, too, is easy to say.
  Give it a rest, wavering,
  as in childhood, day and night,
  as wavering now you wake.

Nothing has passed except the look
  of the recent dead, fresh
  in the distance. In their place
  is the rubble you trample.
  Nothing has passed but their warm,
  woeful eyes, the pupils idle.

Today is the day long ago,
  when, looking close at a loved one
  as if from a great distance, you saw them
  one day, far away.

CIVILTY

"I can't come to see her," the cousin
I'd had a boyhood crush on but hadn't seen

in decades, says at the end of the line. "I know"—
but how knowing, I don't know—

says a voice that is mine
to a Renee whose age and name

are my sister's, the same.
The mouthpiece moistens; I crane

to listen. "I can't bear to see her like this."
"I understand. I'd feel the same if she wasn't my sis."

"I want to remember her . . . as she was . . ."
I listen, and let it pass.

"Like when we were kids, you know?"
"I know."

"We were . . ." catching her breath, "so close. We . . . ," pause,
"were sisters," I fill in. "Yes!" she says.

Memory casts a light on those years
like stars seen here

where light-speed hasn't caught up with
their eons-ago imploded death.

Sundown smears like melting crayons,
but sparing that suffocating smell of a paraffin oven.

"It's o.k.," I say, running out of civilities.
"Thanks, Jackie," shrinks me to childish days.

The trees across the way are winter-thin;
their bare tops tossing in a wind

this moment memory is made, cast
on a mote in a sky cold and vast.

Up in the Air

Shocked to see your face white
as your stubble
after bouts of radiation,

so drained and gaunt
it could have brought out the Jewish
mother in Yasser Arafat,

now cruising at thirty thousand feet sharpens
my view of what I just left,
making clear: In the face

of what's in front of our eyes, the never-ending
fact of the ever-impending end,
memory's a toy; that laboratory

of inventive revising can't hold
a candle to the moment's call.
Blossom or blindfold,

when one we love is about to leave,
grief has arrived out of the future
and set up house,

as Rembrandt in old age
painted his portrait, muddy
shit, piss, and corruption.

Time and nature grow us
into pieces of disfigured indignity.
In it we see what we intended

would never have happened,
and what failed to happen
would have been no better

than what did.
All that is behind us now.
Perhaps everything is behind us now.

Late Prescription

I don't believe God is dead; I believe
God *is* death, whose calling
card is cancer; who cancels our many
small debts with one
                    big theft.

Write what heals,
write what heals,
write what heals
on the heels of what wounds,

or else no good, no good
in the bloodstream, it does
no good; nor eye turned
on her last breath, nor to ask
Death out
from behind the oxygen mask.

To tell of instants
she was and is now
adrift in, is to hold to wreckage, hoping
it floats.

Told, it would have to be
told in a language that lives by busily
dying, that lures its prey
by giving itself away.

Time talks
heart-attack. Her heart talked
time out. Now less than silence
takes it up in pigment and spore,
and in hived tissue builds from surfeit of chaos so
grotesque you have to scramble
to confuse your wits, avert
your eyes, and turn your back

to go on living and not stare, frozen, dumb.

HARVEST MOON, HUNTER'S MOON

Thin as a hairline drawn by the sign-painter's liner
on the show-window glass he can't press
his weight on were the last years
we scoured the medical journals for one
new trial drug after another,
to be ahead of the doctors . . .

                          Now my ear bends
to listen to the god in the ground
you used to plant a seed in, and soon
would emerge a bud barely
green our Stone
Age ancestors pruned.

                          Harvest
moon, full, bright, broad
light over the valley of the shadow
of the living landscape picked clean
for the hunter's clear shot.

                       It laps your heart; with honey-
tart tenderness, woos.
That's the job we do, for room and board,
for the one who wants you

to love him enough to die
of him.

      Don't let his sleepy look fool you;
his dogs have legs that outrun
and make of meat, purée.
Knowing that, it's hard to say
you will not beg as you kneel
to feed him, with rage in one
hand giving way
to rapture in the other.

REQUIEM FOR RENEE

I.
Dawn draws sleepless, raw eyes
to a day where the dark stays all day,
and late September leaves dance on
their own graves.

Renee is no more.
Though she calls
and cries for Mother
Morphine, it's the drug calling

"Come to me who am
painless, boundless, endless . . ."
The anger of the terminally ill
against those caring for but unable

to ease them, and their final litany:
"I don't care anymore."
I give her a sip of ginger ale
to moisten her lips.

"Excuse me," she murmurs when she burps.
And what about the dread in her eyes
when the storm knocks
out the house's power?

2.

Near the end, when things are clear
but unrepairable,
what we had hoped to forestall
we wish would hurry. We wait

with such patience, you could say we wait
with abandon . . . and what we have abandoned
is time, no more
now than what's already over.

3.

In all of autumn's fading, rotting, falling—
a single death is a footnote, if that.
But the larger is not more real
than the small; in death, scale falls away.

Now her leaving brings the unapproachable
nearer, more near to the threshold
of the corridor of corridors
we had not prepared any feelings for.

THE FACE OF THE DYING

The face of the dying, the look
Of slow worms knit:
Ill found, ill fit.

Pain finds a way.
Pain has a way
Finding easy

Prey to stalk. A walk
In the park. Tired arms
Set down what heartache

Romances. Everything
Down to the wood of the bed
Creaks like the key in a lock.

Sunset's opal is going down
Behind the evergreen never not
Standing, arms outstretched, spiral

Branching for Christmas candy.
Underneath the sun's umbrella,
In night's fatigue, to have

Made it this far, and hate it
Enough to want to have it shatter
And made better (the earthquake

Spared, the launch unhurried),
So at the last, we might
Inhale what's buried.

Wandering Moorings

Of blues, the blue of the sky, vaster
than the sea, surely has been here
longer, though maybe not forever . . .

Of catastrophe, though, you have
an idea: loved ones the world
is being emptied of

even while there's time
on the shelf, time to rest, time to enjoy,
time to waste today (we're living it),

though she wouldn't be
given any . . . just enough
time to be asleep in. Just that

alive! In memory's choosing
to favor one of many
claims for attention, I am going

to choose recalling her laughter and delight,
her mouth wide open
with appetite, like an eye with second sight,

which this moment
now is again
catching sight of.

CONVERGENCE

The little girl with lively ironic eyes
looks so much like her grandmother
did at her age, I'm not sure who
I'm seeing, and the instant makes
no difference: two faces fold into one.

Her mother's mother,
gone these last five years,
and she, could be twins.
I'm beamed up, seeing them overlaid
in a loopy overlap of parallel planes, down
to the tell-tale dimple in the smile:
the slyer the humor, the deeper the dimple.

After youth and age, daydream and debris,
we're the sheer
slip shaken off
from the shoulders of a sultan's daughter.

PART 3

A Glow

To enter the darkness and be dazzled,
you buy a ticket, the house dims, and a beam
of concentrated light gleams like a star.
Instantly, the messenger arrives, a radiance
stared at so intently, like a soul being
emptied of its contents for the new inflow,
and disappears into those who are looking
in a dream of transfixed sight. Nothing of
the messenger remains behind but what is left
in mind. Even the glutted can feel
needy, and the greedy, kind; and all can
be loved to death. Angels flying spaceships
can rescue angels falling into a net. But, after
all, the epic showman asserts direction
be restored with a mighty crash. Gravity's
greatest feat is hitting the ground.
Outside, sunlight makes the day
green, for which, in moonlight, we
pray that the window we see through
tomorrow show blue, and if not exactly
airborne, that the blink of an eye
in broad daylight retrieve a glow.

CHANCE ENCOUNTER

You could have been any young man I passed
on the street, since seeing you when you were born
twenty-seven years before was also my last.

What if you were the one this time
who, appraising me, approached and cut me off
at the corner? What if I misread your sign

to mean you were another speedy, tough
punk hustling to sell some dope, or worse?
What if (my worst fear) I'd had enough

and we argued, traded words, traded blows?
The inventory of invective, once begun, has no end.
And what if—adrenalin pumping—about to throw

a final punch, one that'd find
the vital spot, in a sudden dawning—
a sickening stun—it comes to mind:

the lost son could be anyone?

HEEDLESSLY GREEDY

Older now than he was when I left home, more
and more my father's weariness
wears me: his shuffling heaviness
on legs that'd look sinewy and slender

on a young man's frame; heavy, not in weight, but each
slow step nightly up flights fixed in sound.
As a Siberian tiger, coat turning white, paces the ground,
anticipating snow, I turn and reach

in the boy I was for the elderly man who
would be no older now
than he was then, whose absence allows
me to be present here. So

heedlessly greedy are boys, I did not then
care what indignities he had to endure
alone, in secret, nor was I aware
how time hurried on, and old men

scarcely have time to get
details of their debasement right, or to learn
what no amount of regret can gain-
say back, nor undo, nor re-do in light

of the enormity of unlived life
childhood held, that swells to critical mass.
Remorse—its time long past—
grows from roots in night as we leave

day behind, and out the window of our room:
fog and clouds, and beyond, a deeper sky lends
a glimpse of stellar darkness without end,
as we outlive the century in which we were born.

WAILING WALL

The muffled, ticking tread of the wall clock
I mistake a moment for my father's steps
slowly climbing the five flights
after working late in the core of the rotting Apple . . .

Each mounting step, more a shuffle
than a step; more slur than shuffle . . .
Each night I'd hear its sliding snare-
drum cadence, killing time
as time was killing it.

               From this distance,
his bent back is part of the universal wailing
wall, not that ancient ruin in Jerusalem,
but the bowed backs of manic-for-Messiah
black-clad rowers rocking for their lives before it.

After he'd slowly wash up, I'd see
his fingertip-grooves worn smooth and silver-
sheened from the coins passed through,
as if his beating heart—awake or asleep—
were still counting. His daily, cautionary
"Make money in due time, but don't *do* time
for making money," his mercantile mantra,

was to be only half fulfilled: True,
he wasn't doing time, but wasn't making money, either.
Time was doing him.

Our eyes, about to meet, would turn away.
When eyes have not met, nothing real has happened.
At dinner, we were the graves of the animals we ate.

Old Man

Face crisscrossed chock-
Full of lines as a butcher's block,

In his eyes you came to know
A loneliness of pride turned into

What sons learn only too late:
The anguish of fathers that

Becomes an indignant solitude whose chart
Is the cardiogram of a broken heart.

What those eyes revealed of regret
I will not live long enough to fathom or forget.

An hour that waited for me
Was, for him, the dust of years already

Gone. Pleasures clamoring to be repeated
Were, for him, a row of baited

Snares the years denied any savor to.
His gaze, that had held long ago

A ghostly look, had now lost
Even that. To count the cost

Was not the task of time, or to weigh,
Or stop, or look the other way.

There is no call for us to follow,
But we go.

On the Perch

From migratory throats salt holds
the key to, dawn's birdcalls strike and scatter
jot-notes, cracks in a shell's dull glow
that break the silence.
                              On the perch
of seven decades, having reached
an age closing in on the limit of change,
to build a bridge, it must be from the straw
that survives of the things and times lived,
the places they happened in, now empty
of what was done there.

The tall Northern trees could freeze
a person in their tracks
with what they could tell
of what passed under; and of the dead,
who have all eternity
to grow beautiful.
                              As a man
telling of his father will look
like him while speaking, we are
not who we think we are; we are
what ends. Impossible to grow old
so quickly?—The future starts

producing the impossible. Did we
ever leave home— or there now
more than when we lived there?
The dream of what could be seen
if the window were opened
is never what is seen
when the window is opened.
Rothko, trying to imagine the color
of his blood, leaves a light to see
what his closed eyes opened to: black
on gray, night on the moon.

At sundown, the sky's striated red
rock-face shows what the birds whistle into,
probing oncoming dark for depth
enough for their farthest tones,
like twigs thrown against an enormous bell,
before the hood closes over.

OVER

In the way turned clods of earth appear
to enlarge the barren space their
sodden chunks of broken ground were
held in, unturned, there-
by enlarging what we'd other-
wise pass without notice, remember
those days, always summer, come to repair
us kids—white-bread bodies, fevered brains—bare
for the sun's melted butter,
and enlarge our dimmed capacity for pleasure
after numbing months of winter. . . .

In heat prolonged as a solar flare,
the great calamine ocean of desire
thrashed with crowds of eager swimmers.
High noon glare
dried our wet hair, like an instant cure
in the future's favor. The weather
was our mother, master, our
bodies bare
survivors in a prism's heat. Everywhere,
female arms, legs, breasts in halters
on the street, the beach, near-
naked flesh, swelling surrender.

Sweat, lotion, oceanic tar
wafted in from briny sea-water
which remembrance can only stutter
here.
        Not as near
as you'd wish, not as far
as to disappear,
what makes you think you could better
do over, or could love them more
than when they were
with you together—
father, mother, sister,
(stroke, cancer, cancer)—
you older, they as they were?

To My Friend

In spring, a ripple of desire
wrinkles old faces, rekindled
promise banked in embers . . .
summertime dusk in the mellow
tone of Brahms's last clarinet trio,
the smoky, achy solo,
amber autumn sound
I listened to with Carl Rakosi
one sunny day in his apartment
in the foggy Sunset District.

Barely five feet tall, he
and his hi-tech speakers,
the same height.
If we had it to do over again,
we agreed, we'd be composers.
At his hundredth birthday celebration
I asked if I could use a line
from his poem about telling one
"with the missionary eye"
at the Holocaust Memorial to
"Drop dead!" I had meant
for an enemy; it soon happened
to my friend.

THE GOULDBERG VARIATIONS
— (Glen Gould playing Bach's Goldberg Variations)

Opening so often as he does

a simple theme laying out discrete bare notes
he will build on chromatically with more

and more algebraic variations until a solid
resonating grid launches into the monumental,
at the fingertips a pulse of widened intervals, one

and one, a rocking two-three-four spare spiral-
ing aria rising, answered by four descending, four
scale steps descending eight measures, simple, stately, un-
folding triads foreshadowing an eight-fold skipping

doubled to a trill cascade, thirty-two notes
aiming their tonic tones at the heart.
No sender but the notes, no message
but the measure present in every guise and counter-
part hinting at a branching beyond telling—vast

passacaglia fleshing out a polyphonic chorus perpetually
advancing and bounding away to dovetail into one
inevitable wave breaking forward and back, re-

filling the space just emptied. Fixed:
a star's orbit, fueled by a formal burning at the core . . .

Thunder like a torn drum rides the ruts ignited
at breakneck speed, a force of flutter-notes,
slashing overtones, spider-fingering
the white-and-black-ivory web

interwoven with germinating irritants. Beneath
the song, a skeleton; sweat, and reward
for sweat: bread and pears and new

thread from the spindle we spun from, the bird-
throated winds severed by good-bye, and the rangy

call of beginning, before ending.

PART 4

Waving to Normal

Friends now speak more cordially to one another,
in tones more consciously yielding, tender, and after

near-nova disaster witnessed,
have to call on more than good times past

to carry them through the undying
hum inside, sounding

so whispered, subdued, few perceive
as lament. So much we have

to catch up on that laughter has not
demolished yet.

         Had enough
awakening for one day? Is the fiery stuff

sucked through open-air infernos flesh-
infused enough? Is the ash-

swarm chirping cicadic distress calls
of firemens' locator signals

eerie enough? Are you surprised
as a stroke victim, face pressed

against the shower stall,
staring at the fall

of a waterdrop's
globe as it stops

on a tile, the way
a drug knows

where it's needed,
and goes? To heed

the urgency of this
side is to grant there is

no other side; that only here
are the words for whose sake we hear.

And in the garden, at sundown,
where each fractal leaf's etched black on

pale blue only the sky can contain, warbler
alternates with chainsaw, running water

with plosives. Before it ignites, the unthinkable
is news just waiting to be scooped. While

old men are running the world
into the ground they'll soon enter,

their sacrificial song, blown
into our heads in such tones

of sanctity, you feel
you've just been blessed. Soon as you tell,

between breaths, of another loved one's
death upon the recent rest, is as soon

as you know how, for everyone, wounds—
though different—mean the same. Home-

coming is knowing, and having,
though late, a share in the grief that brings

things to a crawl.
The personal

show is over;
the further

cost of knowledge now
that ash and afterglow stare through

the charred lids of "the actual,"
the clay lips that call.

Today will be long ago
when the monuments arrive that are on the way.

Then as Now

At the window, the world
pouring the first bright
sunshine in late winter, earth
calling in its markers . . .

                    Leaf by leaf,
under the lemon tree's canopy,
I was working my way
from the underworld, drowsy, doped
on hope of daylight, seeing
that my eyes were taking a beating
lately, and often blurred.

I had to wake a minute to see
that green was an occupied country;
the streets a theater of random terror;
the ocean, black slick, covered
the wading birds; and stranded faces
on ledges and rooftops, stared, shorn
of everything but ruin.

I wondered if I could trust my senses;
I begged them to make sense. I pleaded
to a father professed to be merciful

an appeal that granted him ears
to hear while knowing he didn't.
For his sake fanatics lay waste
to the present.

I held my breath to hold time
from flowing, and wished no passing—
just the interval—as I did as a boy,
when sunlight that poured then
as now took my breath away.

THE GROUND RUNNING

Rockets gouge the refugees' rooftops;
Céline's rant calms me. . . . reassuring sign
in the same world sanity stops
at the shrine men kill for, in Palestine.

Rabbis rock, mullahs rail;
the call to arms packs stadiums;
God is great as the weight of stockpiles.
Time, growing ripe for delirium,

chews August evening's copper rays
to apricot shoe leather, full-
flavored sunset all the way
down the horizon's throat. In thrall

to the spider I see weave
in twilight its schizy silk-
string purse around a lemon bud, in the sieve
of silence I hear my cats wail for milk's

elixir, and in the garden nosedive deep
in the rose-well, where paradise dwells. . . .
It doesn't look like the farther you leap
or steeper you fall

leaves anyone freer at the end. All
hooded eyes that see our way as no way
of theirs—our arrogance, waste, rapacity—call
on the atomic angel cutting his way

through a field of the living to reach another
level not lived yet, other than to rush
to a briefing room to make far-
distanced death acceptable. Bush,

Ashcroft, Rumsfeld, Cheney, Rice—
coup d'état Crusaders going terror
one better than terrorists—prophesy
(having set in motion) our worst fears.

There's all you need to see and hear in the little
that's heard of what's not being said,
to know there's near nil
enough time—hitting the ground running—Lord,

for us who kill
for you; who die
of you. Still,
it must be hard for you—

looking out for us who can't steer
to any end but slaughter. What's begun,
doesn't end: there
being no ends,

only means . . . which means: meaning well,
we unleash disaster. Having enough,
some day, grown tough, we'll
be better off

without you; better hands at the game.
Some day you'll be fit for a museum.

The Steel Veil

Spreading along with the wind
out of the president's mouth,
desolation, even where there's no dying

going on. Road rage, fraud, price wars, polluted
spin: *that* is peace!
We come to it

as if we'd been away,
new victims
displacing the old

from their desert stone
and sands afloat
on seas of oil.

And those dropping rations
on children they have not
bombed yet—have they

mothers, wives, children, home?
Is someone having a childhood
on those streets?

So let the eyes of orphans swell,
and the widows hiss at us
as they eat our bread

behind veils heavy
as the steel
veil of empire.

History, playing out,
doesn't look like history
being made, but each day's

increasingly incredible
news is increasingly
credible nightmare.

"How far do we have to go
to look for calm from the slaughter;
to take the children on safari,

not return home to put their little
bodies in the ground?" Deep
in the bottom of your heart,

where neutrinos run
you through with ghostly
bullets. Is it any wonder

we fear how we'd fare
in full-scale disaster?
Or would the very lostness

that loosens the mind
free it
to see afresh

the very world it's been
freed from? Deep
in the bottom of your heart,

where there's everything you know
can't come with you;
the bottom of your heart

is not deep enough.

MONEYTHEISM

About to hear more of the incredible
that a sane mind can bear,
like the shore drawing tidal waves from afar

to hear what they have to say,
off the scale comes
a tsunami of viciousness

out of the mouths of those in command.

The bottom line, from under the table,
dangles moon-money
to a family holding its last loaf of bread.

For them, and such as them,
there's no exaggerating the terror
of feeling abandoned at the end.

Everyone, at some time,
gets to be a Jew. I do; and so
will you: if not by birthright,

by being born.
At some time, each must face
the face they're in. This time,

Palestinians are the new Jews,
just as, standing still, we journey
from one instant to another.

The body and the world
wormed with journeying woe. Whatever—
Ha-shem / Allah / the Holy Ghost—

God has to go.

WEATHER REPORT: BAGHDAD BURNING

1.

A little less sparkle in the sunlight;
A little less dazzle in the rays;
A little less sway in the heat of the day
After the heavens rain
Human beings like living torches
Onto the billowing street. . . .

2.

Inuits know the weather is our master.
I'm taking my time with disaster;
I'm trying to make the most of
My master, trying to get the weather right.
I'm starting with September.
It looks right now like I'm in the lap
Of luxury, not to mention the luxury
Of time I'll lap up later, faster.

3.

Summer days, like the tribal-scarred
Girls of Lagos sticking their tongues out
At us in welcome, no longer
Ease toward us and out

Of their flour-sack skirts dyed with juices,
As Indian summer heat huddles, closing down,
And, hazing the horizon, crowds of cumulus
Settle like sailors in their bunks.

4.

Now, in the approach to
Sobering October, a wind stirs
A chill we'll soon be leaning
A shoulder against; a little more
Shade and leaf-sway, a little more
Shadow piling deeper, denser,
For the long haul.

5.

While Baghdad burned,
I wrote my me-moi; memory's fiction.
I see my father, who, alive said little; or not
Exactly see, but spy his look through grinding
Teeth, as in life, in mute lament, his birthplace burning.
He stands in a pressed suit against a night
Lit red with rockets. For all the little sound he makes,
He might as well be alive!

6.

Now that words come slower, harder, plainer,
Than when I was a wooer, woollier, windier,
Listen up: "Even nightingales run out of luck
After building their nest and, singing,
Give their best, only to have crows
Take over, caw and clatter, and leave
Behind their fecal matter;
Only to have (with all due contempt),
Instead of a savior risen,
A president who belongs in prison."

7.

I'm riding unsteadily on the rails
Of rhyme toward what even failing
Eyes can't fail to see, time
And again, when the luxury of
Later has no future.

ARCHEOLOGY

An ashen black crust coats the white
dome and blossoming cherry trees of the Capitol:
empty, abandoned museum.

My friends, let us understand this
stench in the full reach of its vileness.

The visible we are made of
rears on its hind legs
at the jeering whistles of the invisible
hoots from hell. Anything can
veer you into that harrowing
smell. Here, a coup; there,
a tornado. We are allowed
little leeway to muzzle
the running mouths that excrete
what dogs do.

The tongues that bay
of promised bliss are dust; they call
it spring: how, one hand in another,
we'll mine the gold we'll find
at the rainbow's end. Dust
it grinds, and the fallout
is taking up all breathable space.

VILLANELLE

I cut my jaw on the blade
Of politics: the art of madness
In formal dress. Soon, I curled

My way to the top of a tree made
Part flesh, part veil, all hiss.
I cut my jaw on its jagged blade.

Below, history was busy as it hurled
Bodies where we had lain. Your dress
Was all that was left where we had curled

For dear desperate breath in a world
Our bodies craved for the caress
We first feel as we cut our jaw on the blade,

And the instant before we see the blood.
The exquisite edge of that dread kiss
Draws me on to cut my jaw curled

Around the cream of the crop made
Of flesh, the sensate harvest on the abyss
I cut my jaw on, the whiplash blade
Of the world in which we're curled.

Smoking Gun

As a body in the rain will forget it's dust
(Forget it, if you're in Baghdad; dust, there,
Forgets the body was ever wet),
And summer days trail grains of sugar
Jains sprinkle on the ground for ants,
Now September rays contract green days
To gray, as war's shrill whistle blows
Children at play outside of earshot, away.

In the house that is half
Winter Palace, half
Heart of darkness, the destruction
That passes for creation stirs him
More than the mistress he does not have,
More than the wife he does. Outspread
Hands against his chest are a mesh of
Body armor against being born.

Quietly writing, inwardly yelling,
I may be mining for meanings that were never meant.
As is my way, my oxygen is cursing:
I'm breathing and cursing, cursing
And choking (though I've quit smoking!)
I curse the day the bush gave

Partial birth to body parts—wormy
Lips, simian sneer. I waste a curse on

Breath busy having other people dying.

From outer space, the globe's
Swirling blue mouth
Is a smoking gun.
Aliens beware.

Sentence

My reign will last
as long as this sentence
in a language I would make
go on after, for power
has no wish to end no
matter who translates
from me to my crown,
from my teeth to their gold,
from my gold to the straw
you lay in and collude
in my power to harness
your interests to mine,
like the long-ago sunken
light of summer lost
at sea, or fading in a glance
that finally meets itself
over foundations you dig for
as the tide goes out and
the waters return and fill
with your enemies you have
no time to stone or see
their heads roll and I make
this in the people's language
that sleeps with them

and dreams for them and wakes
in them, and what they have
lost I have led them back to,
though these words may be
erased or translated as sounds
that flap in the dark inhabited
by agents who don't speak
except in code that gets mixed
in transmission so as to be
later disavowed in the open
gates of righteousness I stride
through over my enemies, and
which like a carapace closes
around them, bottled flies
in muddy autumn puddles,
with winter close behind,
and the fabled King of
Kings, older than seasons,
grins our worst fears and looks up
from the sentence he reads
as I mount the scaffold he
is famous for, with that vast
laughter that lasts longer,
louder than mine
ever did

A Valentine

In my seventy-first year, with a steadily growing list
Of medications, I need delirium doubled
About as much as another son of a Bush Administration.

I have a problem with that; also with airplanes
Breaking open, raining the people inside into
Human remains falling out of the sky.

For now, being alive is sunny-
Side up in this hour I raise the cup
That is a cabbage rose, spiked petals breaking out

Into full prickly snout. This Valentine's Day,
Mr. President, think about the hearts you have kept
From beating. They are bonding

Into a bouquet blackening in wait
For yours; for which I raise this rose to you,
That its aromatic attar turn to tar

the toxic heart in you.

H.Q. — Q & A

Is the storm approaching ?	Yes.
Is the last coal in the grate?	It is.
To send the basement and the attic . . .	East and west. Yes.
And the people in it . . . ?	You bet.
And the brightness of the bolt . . . ?	Has bolted. Yes.
If the gate is broken . . . that means . . . ?	It does.
Is that an ultimate or alternative?	Guess.
With no option?	Yes.
To the end of the trail?	Good guess.
Will it be soon or late?	Yes.
Is there a timeline?	Guess.
Youth's runaway randomness?	More or less.
Age's random ruinousness?	Alas.
We'll go in grace or disgrace?	Guess again.
Is there any redress?	Less and less.
Has it only seemed marvelous?	At best.
Meaningless?	At least.
Then shall we curse or confess?	Bless.

PART 5

Everglades

Our lives have all gone down to some river
At times to touch bottom. Sunrise low;
Eyes, drawn out, look, but more

Closely you listen for what's in the shadows,
And smell the air of the sawgrass river,
Where a wildcat's stare roots the doe

In place. Gators in the groves, and from a shack
Smoke changing shape like a sleepwalker
Levitating; shapes the tangled mangroves make.

Once, hitchhiking to work in the fields, I lay down
Beneath a shade tree to rest. Afternoon sun
Drove its fire like iron into stone.

Eyes closed a minute, the shadow of a column
Crossed my lids; held, moved, darkened
Between me and blinding noon;

Then opened, I saw the crosshatch-crowned
Head at eye level; hinged, wide jaws
Not three feet away, eye-slits fixing on

Me the gaze of earliest ancestral terror:
Coiled, shiny yellow-black in full sunlight; my scent
On its tongue it luckily did not care for;

As if a whip that could strike
Came alive: held in mid-flick,
The diamondback recoiled me awake.

An Appointment

I have an appointment with the first of May,
in the council houses of sunflower crowns,
in that early air before anxiety
bites with the mosquito's gluttony

in the slow race to finish the crust
before the mold sets in. I remember
the look flowing out of eyes that warmed
and wished well-being on those who received it.

I have an appointment with those eyes
that look like their brains are shining through,
to find with that look as many as I can.

Someone's Dream

There's a light in early May that opens
the fog-gray atmosphere like a ray
widening an aisle in the hallway
to the sun, and spreads being alive
beyond anyone's power to withhold.

It coats the bark of trees, glossy, mossy
stripes of fur, and draws, from the deepest
pores in the wood, primeval sap and light
on the same plane, a honey-hued moment
wiped of memory, which itself will be
remembered, added to the sum
we inhabit that's been held
in safekeeping from earlier springs.

If infinite space makes everything
possible, existing somewhere, and time,
being infinite too, plays out
every variable in some near or distant realm,
someone's dream somewhere is coming true.

SCENT

No one but a god
could smell like the sea,
a god who tosses us
to the fish and the fish
onto our plates, and a taste
that reaches you only
now, in the salt savor
of open space. We are
parts of a world full of
forests and deserts and
creatures we tame and eat
and light the night that's light
years wide, flecks
on the observation deck
heading for altitude's perpetual
green light, set on playing
in the sandbox of outer space,
leaping and lazing, gravityless,
where through the wide bay
window spreads a stellar Dust
Bowl for our efforts, less lyrical
than landfill, showing itself
nowhere empty of the hand
that comes down harder than
thunder and commands us to fall
in love with it.

Annals of the Mute

With growing numbers and frequency
of whales and seal pups washed ashore,
it's clear we're witnessing the death wish
of creatures who previously had no wishes,
only instincts. Imagine evolving
to being able to wish, and wishing for
extinction, which may take a while to fulfill.
In the meantime, your cat gives you that
slow, low-lidded look at your complicity
no matter how much you protest—
like the torero to the charging bull—
that you're a vegetarian; that you wish
we may be long gone before the fish
and fowl and four-legged creatures
are no more; that you think
it's about time the big trees,
which have taken in sunlight
the deepest, and cast the longest
shadows, and drunk enough rain,
and provide the paper, are owed
a chapter and should have a say
in the as-yet unwritten
annals of the mute.

Rose in Scorpio

Time to turn
Clocks back again
For time
To gain

An hour
On eternity now
That light lowers
Early in Scorpio,

And glossy leaves caress
Blood-rose rays
In a vacantness
The slate sky is

Blackboard for, broad
Enough to write
Justice, code word
For Holy Writ's

Sanction of slaughter. How
Rare
To see sorrow
Starving anywhere;

Even less rare, wasted
Women, swollen
Babies at their breast,
Famished at the fountain

Of gorging flies.
By the time the green
Lemons on the trees
Yellow, fruition's season

Is over. With age,
At the bottom
Of crumpled cartilage,
Illness leaves less from

Which to draw. Without
Petals from the solar rose,
There is no light
Of sanity. And as close

To a home-
Grown galaxy as the
Roses come, their bloom
Soon withers away;

And the hummingbird whirrs
Toward budding flowers,
To gardens and weather
Other than ours.

A fishbone cypress
Stands in the sky's
Gullet, which is
All of space.

Here sunset's rust-
Red carpet
Glows, casts
Facets of a fire agate

Lighting a portal
To earth's ages,
Richly raw as primal
Technicolor you'd merge

With if you could. The storm
Of solar wind that reaches
Us as light and time,
In passing, touches

And ignites; each
Day's brightness flips
Synapse on, a light switch,
Creation's catnip.

All the while,
The sulfurous smell
Of history's rubble
Rolls forth in a ball.

Petals shed to a bald halo:
Rose hips; the zero
Rose in Scorpio
Has had its day,

As winter stretches
Day and night now,
And bitter cold switches
To worse in a flash so

Dear to the gods,
Who dine on
Smoke, who goad
A mob's din

In the ears
Of those who'd rather
Wither in fire
Than one day hear,

Cried from their own throats,
The human horrors
Their prayers have wrought,
As the rose scatters.

HYMN
— (after *the Rig Veda*)

I do not wish, Lord of Air,
To go down to the heavy house of clay.
Be gracious, Lord, and spare.

Since on increasingly faltering legs I fare,
Body more mutinous than in my younger days,
Be gracious, Lord, and spare.

Though thirst was the plaint of your singer
Even as he stood in running waters,
Be gracious, Lord, and spare.

Though I have been a conspirer,
Tirelessly conspiring with my pyre,
Be gracious, Lord, and spare.

A liar and destroyer posing as a creator,
I have beaten my ploughshare into a scimitar,
Be gracious, Lord, and spare.

Though the days disappear like markers
Of a road that is no longer there,
Be gracious, Lord, and spare.

As when silence is grazed by a wing's stir
When a bird sings in the night air,
Be gracious, Lord, and spare.

To the universe belongs the dancer.
Let me push off with my foot
And a new road be there.

Be gracious, Lord, and spare.

Unhinged

All those still holding to their youth,
Nod your head. God loves
Cropping the daffodils
And the flowering rose
That buds and rots and drops
Its petals on its own
Grave.

As one grows older, poetry becomes less
Bankable, more bedrock: depth and
Rust as the blue world blurs.

But, so help me, I no longer believe
Art is worth sacrificing a life for.
I'm not on a mission
Sent by anyone. I'm not
Searching for myself,
Or you, or anything; only to slip-
Slide through the waste
Tirelessly greased by the blade's
Blood flow.

Sing or grieve
What goes

Of what's received.
The living know death
In name only. . . .

And the next myth
Will be no wiser.

Sickbed Redux

Sickbed is a better place
Than many to review your state
Of health, or lack thereof . . . space-
Yawning window looking out

On a receding world growing faster
And farther away, as swift
Stimuli on the surface—air,
Light, speech, touch—drift

Out of reach, to the bottom
Of thought, to thought
With a clarity seen from
Below, where your caught

Aging face in a mirror
Silvered with years is covering
What?—a child's heart? A mirror
Holds many faces, but no heart. Hovering

Likeness released from earthly weight,
Blankness, too, is part of the bargain,
As is the autumn-aching note
Of Brahms's last clarinet solo. What's broken

In disillusion was kissed
So deep its curses can't be peeled off.
Now all your noble vows must
Vie with their larval undertow and the rough

Bitterness the mortally ill feel
Entitled to, like a bird near
The end of flying. We're not able
To know if God cares

Whether what grows is a child
Or cancer; or if, with knife and fork, we lift
A rainbow from a salmon's scales, or build
Spaceships for the reddest shift,

Or, ebbing grace note, we end in gravel.

The Buddha Sends His Regrets

Part the curtains and the light pours in . . .
March winds' bright brusqueness
gust away whatever was burnt today

or long discarded, the rust-needled
Christmas tree lying, a hulk of flaking
fishbone by the fence.

The dust glitters, but not for long.
Though the old year's losses fade
in how today feels, all that lives

in the world we call ours are born of
molecules in motion to leave it: this
garden, and grief

to haul it away. That's all
you can say about the visible:
it vanishes in a sky vast and empty

as before there ever was grief,
or an eye to cry it.
Here, where the west comes to rest,

the Buddha sends his regrets
weighing no more
than a feather blown from a wing,

light as the silence that waits,
can wait
forever, to whither

the voice that lies and hides,
and does to the mind
what time does to a face.

Sunny Days

Midday as in late summer, though it's barely
Early March, and with the velvety rustle of little
More than skin-and-bone-wings, a warbler
Wolf-whistles the blue loveliness above.

In Berkeley, the sidewalk outside the café is the color
Of the sky. I'm soaking up the sunshine, lapping
A latte, tasting the flakiest croissant au chocolat
In what may be my last meal toward the end

Of the era of unchecked power of the Western World,
While a cherry-sweet chirping in the trees is clearing
Throats of winter. Today, throats are better off
In Berkeley than in Baghdad,

Where in one form or another heat hits
Like a stroke, even where a car-roadside-or-human
Bomb has not. There are so many
Sunny days for death in Baghdad.

The sky above here, as there, though limitless
Beneath which we pray not to suffer
What is made with so much space
To suffer in, is not big enough for me

To feel what a mother must feel
On the street as she turns on her heel
At the sound of danger to her children;
Or before sending one out

For the day's bread, knowing it could cost
The life of one who has breathed

In, through, out of you.

Just this morning, taking a hot shower, I heard,
"This is as close as you will get to being with
Your mother again," and for a second forgot
What dimension I would step out into.

Fast fatiguing, fitful sleeping,
Urgent peeing, eyesight dimming,
Are not good omens for hope,
Since all our hopes suppose

We'll live them healthy.

Instead, a person across the sea
Nightly crumbles before our eyes,
Laying his head like a heart in a vise
For the handler's pleasure.

The weight of multitudes and their gods:
I hate the weight of the gods

Of multitudes, but love heaven's
Silken silence leaving no trail

But sunset's crimsoning sail.
Light dims; cats doze; birds start up their din.
This is the hour I like best, which slides
Slow as a veil over a ravishing creature's thigh,

Who will ravish again tomorrow.

Family and self-preservation aside, my worst fear
In the doomsday scenarios I'm given to lately
Is a quake, nuclear, or terrorist attack,
In which my seven cats scatter

To the four winds; creatures so high-strung,
And still, they're lordly and lethal at once,
Yet whose squinting eyes pain makes
Even the kitten's frightened face shrunken, old.

Where to, then, who have never known anywhere
But home? First, let me sweep the stones
From their path, and pray their killing
Skills thrive on living smells in the grass.

For us, there's the astronomical
Luck in the starlight not stopping.

Fallback Time

Late November's coiling serpentine sunset stretches
Flame behind the hill-crest where winter in the west comes
To rest. Day's light was cold, dim, brief.
From the bay, a muffled foghorn brays. An hour

Extra for greed to do its work. Justice is tasered, dead
To the world; to lamplight from buried miners' helmets
Bathed in coal dust; to gaudy baubles strung with gifts
In a holiday season that can mine mass murder while partying

On. After seventy, failing eyes squint in a narrow, dim
Space where everything is back-lit
With twilight. At my window, I stay to see the long
Spread: hot red, cool violet, dark blue

Silhouetting the peaks before the hills, the houses, and the trees
Blacken. Closer to
The end, we hold close what we hold,
Whether or not true, that we may go on living

The lives we do, while language rare as sanity lies
Low. Up ahead: the onset of faculties failing,
Loved ones losing limbs, organs, lives. After a few
Years unable to picture their faces, their absence slips away . . .

Death has become less a distant threat
Than never absent.
Three days ago I choked on a vitamin pill
Stuck in my throat before Naomi rushed in

And Heimliched me until it loosened;
Gasping for breath,
I swallowed, gulping lungfuls of air
From far away, from breath's beginning.

Next day, a tanker spilled crude oil into the bay.
The news showed birds on the beach, so saturated
In viscous tar, they could not part their beaks
To breathe. Pity, there is no Heimlich for the birds!

On the other side of the world stripped and slagged,
The screams of tortured men are screams of children;
A refugee woman, wrinkled dry as the ground behind her,
who lost her children to famine and slaughter, is saying

"When two elephants fight, the grass suffers.
We are the grass."

TO THE ORPHEUS OF THE AWFUL

I.

Prematurely, late August leaves fall, curl, crisp as chips;
Sunsets moving south, daylight briefer,
Darkness sooner, air chill, and a humming

Shadow not yet at final rest, smaller than a sparrow,
Bigger than a bee, buzzes flicks
On the beige stucco wall, as you take a rest

From watching the coming phase of the terrible
Toys for the children, with evening's lament
From everlasting larynx wailing over the hills.

Burning towers; sounds of tribes crying;
Rivers of cries as real as any river
You drown in, you take a rest from

Evening's larynx, everlasting lament;
Eyeballs sore as flayed backs and feet
In hegiras through desert heat; a slow,

Steady stamping of feet, a muffled tom-tom
Risen from Earth's drum by multitudes
Longing to rise off the ground, or sink

Underneath, who cannot live
Upon it; who forge chains from the straw
They inherit and, parched for Paradise,

Mix their blood in its sand, no longer slaves
To their meat, while we take another crack
At making Iraq pita-flat.

2.
See the cat. See a thousand years of it
Stroll out of the weeds, veiled
In a chador of spider's lace.

Swatting flies, it twists in midair, twirling
Lariat, claws and tail,
Even as your eyes dim and your legs lift dead

Weight. Smell the woodsmoke of autumn
Nowhere near. See the tops of trees
Lit by sundown glow like blondes

With dark roots. As soon as it sinks
Behind the hills: dark, not a sound,
No one around, quiet as a shark

Prowling an empty aquarium.
Each part of the darkness is
The whole. In the realm of

The not-for-long, everyone is afforded
A partial view of the show before
They're swept out of the stalls.

And you?—You're several
Layers of time
Ago removed.

In decline, powers weaken,
And all weaknesses, tested, worsen
And win, as you waken to a night

That almost finishes you.
Help
Give one last push

To the falling wall, and sweep
Out the stall
To the endlessness, alas, that ends.

COLOPHON

The Steel Veil was designed at Coffee House Press,
in the historic warehouse district of downtown Minneapolis.
Fonts include Caslon and Blakely Light.

FUNDER ACKNOWLEDGMENTS

Coffee House Press is an independent nonprofit literary publisher. Our books
are made possible through the generous support of grants and gifts from many
foundations, corporate giving programs, state and federal support, and through
donations from individuals who believe in the transformational power of litera-
ture. Coffee House Press receives general operating support from the Minnesota
State Arts Board, through an appropriation by the Minnesota State Legislature
and from the National Endowment for the Arts, and major general operating
support from the McKnight Foundation, and from Target. Coffee House also
receives support from: two anonymous donors; the Elmer L. and Eleanor J.
Andersen Foundation; Bill Berkson; the Buuck Family Foundation; the Patrick
and Aimee Butler Family Foundation; Jennifer Haugh; Joanne Hilton; Stephen
and Isabel Keating; the Kenneth Koch Literary Estate; Allan and Cinda
Kornblum; Seymour Kornblum and Gerry Lauter; Kathryn and Dean Koutsky;
Ethan J. Litman; Mary McDermid; Stu Wilson and Melissa Barker; the
Lenfestey Family Foundation; Rebecca Rand; the law firm of Schwegman,
Lundberg, Woessner, PA.; Charles Steffey and Suzannah Martin; the James R.
Thorpe Foundation; the Woessner Freeman Family Foundation; the Wood-Rill
Foundation; and many other generous individual donors.

 This activity is made possible
in part by a grant from the
Minnesota State Arts Board,
through an appropriation by the
Minnesota State Legislature
and a grant from the National
Endowment for the Arts. MINNESOTA
STATE ARTS BOARD

 TARGET.

To you and our many readers across the country,
we send our thanks for your continuing support.

Good books are brewing at coffeehousepress.org